NOVEMBER ENDING

MISHA FEIGIN

Misha Feigin/Dreaming People Publishing
Printed in the United States of America

Front cover photo by Misha Feigin
Back cover photo by David Green

Publisher's Note: Names, characters, places, and incidents are a product of the author's imagination. Locales and public names are sometimes used for atmospheric purposes. Any resemblance to actual people, living or dead, or to businesses, companies, events, institutions, or locales is completely coincidental.

November Ending/ Misha Feigin. -- 1st ed.

Contents

I would like to thank Quinn Chipley for his generous help that allowed me to complete this book and Steven Skaggs for the front cover calligraphy.

I

In the Beginning

THE LINK

...and this other man sneers

keeping his mouth shut

behind my eyes,

I suspect someone else

smiles like an angel behind his,

so when I try to make sense of

a wind bursting into an open window

in my study full of dusty books and

piled papers covered with wry scribbles,

I have to go through all of us

like a nun thumbing her prayer beads,

muttering some obscure verses

passed from one silence to another...

THE SQUAT

It is just a room

people go through

shading a skin or two,

An idle eye

does not disturb the dust

blanketing edges and corners,

Spiders and ants traverse

the lace of ceiling cracks,

the map of the unnecessary,

I draw a star

on beams of oblique light

percolating through broken windows,

A funnel begins to form…

ANTIDOTE

How much protection

can walls of books and records

provide against the bleached world

where determined men and women

lunge with knives, swing axes,

pull triggers or activate detonators?

What kind of serenity

can aged defenses ensure

when digital data ooze

into shrinking reality

through legions of ghostly

bluish screens invading

every room or pocket,

ready to flicker, reflecting

in wondering eyes?

I touch the aged bindings,

pulling out a volume of Chekhov.

A Bartok concerto sounds

as good as ever on my stereo.

NOTHING TO LOSE

> *"Anxiety is the dizziness of freedom"*
> *Søren Kierkegaard*

Breaking from restraints

of anything measured,

dispatching oneself

into merging dimensions

of unbounded now –

being there is being

here with every vibration

in each cell

broadcasting presence

into the yielding void.

THERMODYNAMICS REVISITED

Love is a paradox –

the more you give,

the more you have

left to give.

Love grows in every cell

like chlorophyll waiting

to be released into the open

where it belongs –

to condense into nebulas,

to ignite stars, to form planets,

to become a sheltering atmosphere,

where lightning gives life a chance

to crawl out of the soup of elements

spreading in a rage of procreations,

trying every route to persevere,

to carry the spark it was born from

celebrating the metamorphosis

of perpetual return.

VIOLATION (0.999…)

How many stars

have to ignite and

collapse before

a probability

of not being born,

this infinite procession

of nines,

will be ignored

by a victorious sperm

invasion penetrating

a designated egg and

the first cry joins

a symphony of noises

emanating from anything

growing and moving

in the shelter

of the atmosphere?

I move my pen

across a blank page –

one more scribble,

one more sound.

LIBRARY AWAKEN

Resilient, stubborn –

the fresh glass blades

shoot through the cracked

asphalt in a sleepy lane –

just like a few rogue

sunbeams penetrate

a windowpane illuminating

the stirred dust specks' frenzy

around the wall of volumes.

NOISES AND SCRIBBLES*

It's all about

communication –

a swirling monkey ruckus,

a glorious heron dance,

a serene whale call,

an eerie rattlesnake shake,

a squatted cat's hiss,

a scared mouse squeak –

sonic waves shaped by

love, fear and solidarity,

these scribbles you read now

with your lips moving

transforming the ink blots

into noises you can pass

to the other –

the ever changing flow

of symbols washing over

the unfathomable outside

where every vibration counts.

*Words Richard Portly uses to describe language
in his book " Contingency, Irony and Solidarity"*

COLLECTION

"What can be shown cannot be said."
Ludwig Wittgenstein

A fresh word hatches

from cracked oblivion

pointing at the thing that

caused it to be pronounced

and pinned to the paper

like an expired butterfly

with iridescent wings

stopped by an avid collector

adoring his treasures

in a quiet, darkened room,

the yellow lamplight

reflects from glass cases

spread on a broad desk,

dusty books crowd shelves

looming on every wall

like decommissioned ships

in some forgotten harbor,

all frozen in the past that

never became the future

in the world of lost

language and wonder.

AFTERGLOW

My stellar twin,

Is he closing his eyes

when I shut mine?

How does this tea

tastes on his tongue?

Do our hearts

pound in sync until

the strings connecting us

shiver and break letting

one more chord to escape

in the warped dimensions

where no time and space matter?

I look at the stars

and listen…

BROADCAST

Once inside the body

reaching the bloodstream,

what does the sound become?

Is there an ear in every cell

letting it in – just like sugar and

fat fueling mitochondria engines

powering every turn we make,

making

our breath to taste

sweet in the opening mouth,

sending goosebumps

to cascade across alert skin

forcing that little shiver behind*

to break through the daily crust,

to unfold its petals and antennas

joining the others broadcasting life…

* *"Although we read with our minds, the seat of artistic delight is between the shoulder blades. That little shiver behind is quite certainly the highest form of emotion that humanity has attained when evolving pure art and pure science." - from Vladimir Nabokov's chapter on "Bleak House" in his Lectures on Literature*

PRACTICAL

What are you without

memory - a strange fruit

still walking free

half-sour, half-rotten,

a microbiome carrier with

watering eyes and runny nose

never arguing with a mirror

early in the morning

in a fumigated bathroom.

Nothing to hide means nothing

to show or hold onto except

aching bones and cracked skin

still holding the worn-out flesh

in a recognizable shape,

the essence passing through

unimpeded by forgotten self –

prana in, apana out,

hold your breath,

wait, breathe.

JUST RIGHT

The moment when the fresh

baguette is cut open and

warm aroma permeates the air,

the moment when salted butter

is spread over its porous flesh,

the moment when teeth

bite into the crunchy crust –

a moment innocent enough

to stop the world from spinning.

II

RIDING ALONG

SHORT

Where did it go wrong,

collective memory?

What rogue winds scatter

vestiges of a missing rib,

a murdered brother or

a decomposed film

spilled from a rusted case

in a cluttered store room?

Amnesia cycles roll

washing away the soil

until no more space is left

for anything growing

and the crust get exposed

to fiery blows of cosmic

debris coming from

the same star that birthed it.

COMMODITIES

Thinking in bricks, containers,

sale units – any measurements

useful for the ever expanding

craving for more – not much better

than drinking from a puddle

in a vacant parking lot

flavored with freshly dropped

antifreeze and gasoline,

a few clouds,

still reflect there,

a wind ripples it…

SALVAGE

From a fish digging into

the sand on the bottom

to a frog absorbed

by his mating song,

from waves crushing

against the rough shore

to the rain beating

against the cracked asphalt,

from Bel Canto to bloating,

from consciousness to soupy soap –

anything stirring the flow

makes bubbles

puffing and popping,

releasing oxygen back

into the forgiving atmosphere.

ON BENEFITS OF PRACTICING

Making sharp turns,

doubling the speed

in a split second,

leaping at the trees,

merging with the brush,

melting away with shadows –

all these early techniques

that helped my species

to climb on top

of the food chain

still might work

for anyone hoping

to get through

a holocaust or two.

NO SWEAT

Climbing from fork to fork

on the tree of possibilities

growing out of the second level

of chaos – the one that gets affected

by predictions, so it never can be

predicted - just like the domain of

the quantum cat (a cousin of

the Cheshire one) who finally

makes her choice to materialize

behind a certain door,

perhaps leaving her vanishing grin

in the pre-choice limbo –

not an easy choice for a reasonable

cat always stuck on a wrong side of

the door. What can one gain anyway

by an effort to choose anything

in the vortex of yin and yang?

I throw my fingers on the keys, listen –

waiting for the sound to dissipate.

Another chord. Another silence.

Another turn for a flowing mind.

BY THE WINDOW

A moment immersed

in a mirage of perfection

and a promise of return,

alas - this spring

is not eternal,

neither are you

forever young,

but still,

your senses soak

the incredible freshness

of soft, gray morning

with light drizzle invigorating

everything budding and blooming,

sparrows' and robins' voices

rise to crescendo,

a surprised squirrel scampers

on freshly green branches –

they were still dark yesterday.

And here, by an open window,

you are what you are

sailing through disturbances

until your breath leaves you and

all elements you keep captive

return to the heart of

Whatever-It-Is

propelling our universe

from one Big Bang

to another.

THROUGH DECEMBER

Traversing the waves of
stirring darkness saturated
with cold drizzle, and wind gusts
sending the last surviving leaves
to swirl in the headlights,

Of a late bus, the odd aquarium
rolls along the deserted
downtown strip, its tires
swish spraying water
from invisible puddles,

Swaying softly in the cocoon
of the warm, golden light,
a few black men sit apart,
staring at their telephones,
sharing poverty and solitude.

A young couple walks away
from a closing restaurant,
they embrace, laughing.

Their car beeps. The tail lights

blink cheerfully.

The full moon emerges,

for a moment shrouded

with torn, ghostly clouds.

One more night proceeds

In its merciless glory.

RECURRENCE

Trapped in the same dimension,

sages and fools,

we fulfill our fates craving

for this penetrative touch

of the incomprehensible outside

where the flame that mothered us once

is still burning,

oblivious to the flame we all share,

a flame radiating from irises,

passing from skin to skin,

from ear to ear

until nothing is left

to stop it from becoming the fire.

HOME

*"You never own a cat, you are just
lucky to live with one."*
Terence Dumsbereger

Whatever the reasons are –

you are where you are,

dasein – as one Nazi philosopher

put it – is all you can brandish –

forget about having anything

in the world that has us.

Wanting is the vessel

you are assigned to navigate

in the sea of all things connected

scanning the horizon with your antennae

in search of the sweetest sound.

STORY

A cat leaps upward.

Furious grace erupts.

A frightened bird flies unhurt.

Claws retract. Soft landing.

What goes up must come down,

But what if there no ups and downs,

and solar winds are

the only nourishment needed

for a multitude of creatures

traversing the open darkness,

luminous sails flow

from world to world

in the flux of All-That-Is

punctuated by everything,

still contained by shapes –

Breathing words in a story

telling itself to itself

in perpetual wonder.

IN THE HILLS

Climbing a steep, winding path,
grasping at young trees here and
there, pushing through to the top
just to see another valley
opening in the midst of the endless,
petrified waves of the hills,
green and luring under serene skies,

Longing to remain in this breath,
this moment, craving to have it all
in the never-ending now where
each part is the whole and holy,
now where first stars emerge
in the darkening sky and it's time
to set a camp for one more night.

III

IN SHORT

On a mountain side

challenging the morning sun –

the azalea flames.

Meadow grasses bend

passing the hard winds along,

in wave after wave.

How could it happen –

between the grasshopper's chirrs

the whole world gets lost?

For a few minutes,

a small black bug leads me

down the forest path.

First time in a year

to see what's new on the hills

moving and growing.

What can be better –

becoming all of it

In just a moment!

The first raindrops fall.

The sky's reflection ripples, melts

in a little pond,

the happy frog's song rising

to the rushing clouds.

Is there the best angle

to look at the harvest moon?

Clouds float in awe.

Just for a moment,

a sudden gust shakes the trees.

A cat chasing a stirred leaf

stops disappointed and puzzled:

Is it still the same world here?

OCTOBER SUN

Not fully awake,

still reaching for the other,

so we can dream each other

again.

It's a curtain call:

the gold, golden light

pouring into still air.

Suddenly frozen –

the world outside the window,

then – a shrill bird's call.

On the cracked asphalt,

the sound caught in the broken glass

beams from every shard.

A new day's blessing –

the pale blue October sky,

some trees, shrubs still green.

Cicadas

Sleeping underground

songless, what dreams do they see

for seventeen years?

After the harvest,

trees unbend, free and empty

to face the winter.

An overlooked apple

in the deserted orchard,

a wayfarer's prize.

Last summer fragrance

explodes in a craving mouth.

The glorious crunch.

They faded too fast

on the dusty window glass –

oblique sun letters.

A closed book,

a sleeping bird,

a starless void –

there is no silence.

A stroke of a pen

fending off insanity –

as long as it moves.

A glass of water

in front of my eyes, your eyes –

what a difference!

Gleaming on the dust,

sun runes on the window glass

emerge and vanish.

It is in my palm,

a path to infinity –

a gleaming rain drop.

In the dark thicket,

a starling call is the first

driving the sunrise.

Not blank anymore,

the sunlight spills on a page,

outlined by the ink.

IN DEFENSE OF MONKEY MIND

Jumping left and right,

a spry monkey's better than

no monkey at all.

It's just you, José,

a cup of hot tea, a pen,

and whatever comes.

EVOLUTION

Upright lizards' time –

too late for an asteroid,

they are Space-ready.

The skies are folding

over a sweet prairie home.

The beans are burning

Don't panic, Jovanni –

they are just your wings,

these snowy feathers

carrying you freely

through the stirring air.

Under the bleak gray,

a sea of purple and gold stirs,

the first frost is here.

A silent gray wave

embraces a sleepy town,

a crow calls: resist!

They never doubt it,

squirrels huddling in the nest –o

the sky is still there!

On naked branches,

the drops of silver scattered.

The freezing rain stops.

A single branch alive

on a dark, withered tree trunk,

still pliant, still green.

A morning surprise –

squirrel tracks on the first snow,

December letters.

THE NEW YEAR FREEZE

On a window sill,

a cat is absorbed watching

the great outside film.

The pale sun frozen

in the bleached alien blue.

The warm home blessings.

IV

ENDINGS

In the morning freeze,

a few scattered leaves shiver

on barren branches –

a message to a new spring

from one more imperfect fall.

The fog's shroud vanishing

In the serene morning sun,

a fading palm print

on the window glass,

still cold.

It all might end well –

a confident crow broadcasts

from the naked walnut tree

rising darkly at the edge

of the parking lot

sending ripples through

the thick gray air

blanketing one more

unsuspecting morning.

LETHARGY

Slipping into a dream

deeper and deeper,

chimes ring softer,

eyelids so heavy,

what have I lost

in the listless morass

of the outside?

Gray winter light

oozes into the retina,

blurry contours of things

familiar take shape,

a few shrunken leaves pass

across the window frame

waltzing in the wind,

The puffy cocoon of a comforter

feels paralyzingly cozy,

slow morning fills the room

with more uncertainty,

in a fit of last effort veracity

I threw the blanket aside

and jump into my slippers.

BEFORE A SONG

A low, gray sky

looming through the web

of naked tree branches –

a picture framed by a window,

it's never finished –

this morning, any morning.

Ragged clouds moving in,

two crows flying high,

wordless thoughts slipping

into the rising silence

to emerge as fresh sounds,

it's harvest time.

OVERNIGHT

Swallowing a small park,

a stream turned to flood

brown water tongues grass,

overflows arching bridges;

a duck bobs paddling through.

Punctured by lightning, the

darkness wraps the horizon,

with rain and wind paused,

an opening in torn clouds,

it's so unbearably blue.

A PLACE TO BE

A glorious parasite,

DNA tries all possibilities –

whatever platform it might

use – deep, wide or high,

the whole beast of life turns

morphing into countless species

rampaging mindlessly until

one day a coconut falls on the head

of a certain hunter-gatherer

causing her to drop

a juicy piece of rabbit

onto a smoldering stump of a tree

hit by lightning in the morning,

the determined hominid picks up

her warmed dinner and takes

a good bite – "Uuuh!" Jonny

(or maybe her name was Uoki)

exclaims, full of surprising delight

scratching a bump on her head,

her neurons fire – and the art of

cooking and the history of Sapiens

begins proceeding to the point

where the nebulous consciousness

pops up in the brains of

industrious creatures

powering their relentless climb

to the top of the food chain

where they perch

nourishing the unsalable urge

to consume and conquer

wiping out anything impeding –

whether it grows or moves,

including their own – until

the self-loathing consciousness

won't be able to live with itself

and blasts them out of the future

where some machines and

bacteria still might have

a place to be.

Amor Fati–

not mon amour or

meine Geliebte,

not even tough love.

A one hand clap

is just a tickle –

can you hear the sound

of gods laughing?

a few ripples run across

the impenetrable blue,

the sky pond is smooth,

now you are a frog

that still needs to do

the jumping,

    maybe this time…

GATHERING MOTHER

I walk into the shabby geometry

of cheap apartment buildings,

two-floor dominoes still housing

hopes, joys and despair,

rolling Spanish r's fly around

in place of smoother Russian ones.

Here is the right number,

I come in and climb the steep stairs

still reeking of the carpet disinfectant,

two oversize sneakers guard

the worn out door we pushed

so many times,

I touch the door and wait…

Your vestige waves at me'

from the empty balcony

when I look back passing

through the fence gap

into the empty church parking lot

soon walking along the dirty creek

a few ducks still enjoy.

The gray day envelopes

the sleepy neighborhood infused

with my memories, your memories,

I move my hand slowly

letting one more reality to settle,

I talk to you softly,

Your responses emerge nebulously

in my voice, in your voice -

no farewells or hellos anymore,

I feel a strand of yarn unwrapping

in my chest, a thread you pull gently

leading me through the fog

I am beginning to see.

NOVEMBER ENDING

In a forgotten cemetery,

a rustling vortex of leaves rises

above scattered tombstones

like a swarm of butterflies

morphing with the next gust

into a flock of sparrows dashing

above a crumbling brick wall

across a withered meadow

all the way to a swollen creek

settling on muddy water

on the way

to the Southern Seas –

messages of one more

November ending

ABOUT THE AUTHOR

Misha Feigin was born and raised in Moscow He won the Thomas Merton Prize for Poetry in 2000 and was awarded the Al Smith Fellowship for Creative Nonfiction in 2002. His books include a novel, Searching for Irina, a free style travelogue Tribal Diaries, and four books of poetry, The Last Word in Astronomy, Abraham's Bagel, Skippers in Training, and Cloud Letters. Misha currently lives in Louisville, Kentucky

Misha Feigin is known as one of Russia's premier guitarists. He released two albums on the the state label, Melodiya. Misha has toured throughout North America and Europe and has released fourteen CDs in US, Germany, and Holland. He has released two CDs in Great Britain on Leo Records. Misha shared a stage and recorded with Elliot Sharp, Steve Beresford, Dave Liebman, and Eugene Chadbourne.

For more info visit www.mishafeigin.free-jazz.net